Shelve w/ State
Books

P9-CDJ-301

Chase Branch Library
17731 W. Seven Mile Rd.
Detroit, MI 48235

CH
JUN - - 2004

Michigan
Plants and Animals

Marcia Schonberg

Heinemann Library
Chicago, Illinois

© 2004 Heinemann Library
a division of Reed Elsevier Inc.
Chicago, Illinois

Customer Service 888-454-2279

Visit our website at www.heinemannlibrary.com

All rights reserved. No part of this publication may
be reproduced or transmitted in any form or by any
means, electronic or mechanical, including photo-
copying, recording, taping, or any information stor-
age and retrieval system, without permission in writ-
ing from the publisher.

Designed by HeinemannLibrary
Photo research by Stephanie L. Miller
Printed in the United States by Lake Book
    Manufacturing, Inc.

08 07 06 05 04
10 9 8 7 6 5 4 3 2 1

**Library of Congress
Cataloging-in-Publication Data**
Schonberg, Marcia.
  Michigan plants and animals / Marcia Schonberg.
    v. cm. -- (Heinemann state studies)
Includes bibliographical references (p.   ) and index.
Contents: Forests -- The Great Lakes, sand dunes,
and beaches -- Inland lakes, rivers, and streams --
Swamps, marshes, and wetlands -- Extinct
plants and animals -- Endangered plants and
animals -- People, plants, and animals -- Map of
Michigan.
  ISBN 1-4034-0662-6 (Hardcover) -- ISBN 1-4034-
2679-1 (Paperback)
  1. Natural history--Michigan--Juvenile literature. 2.
Endangered species--Michigan--Juvenile literature. [1.
Michigan. 2. Natural history--Michigan. 3. Endangered species.] I. Title. II. Series.
  QH105.M5S36 2003
  578'.09774--dc22

                                          2003017160

Acknowledgments
The author and publishers are grateful to the
following for permission to reproduce copyright
material:
Title page (L-R) Robert Lifson/Heinemann Library,
Mark Hamblin/Oxford Scientific Films, John Lemk-
er/Animals Animals; contents page (L-R) Robert
Gill/Corbis, D. Robert & Lorri Franz/Corbis; pp. 4,
24 David Muench/Corbis; pp. 5b, 33
Bettmann/Corbis; pp. 5t, 8, 19, 23 Robert
Lifson/Heinemann Library; p. 9 maps.com/Heine-
mann Library; p. 10 Bill Beatty/Visuals Unlimited;
pp. 12b, 40t D. Robert & Lorri Franz/Corbis; p. 12t
Mark Hamblin/Oxford Scientific Films; p. 13 Ron
Austing/Frank Lane Picture Agency/Corbis; p. 14
Lowell Georgia/Corbis; p. 16 Dale C. Spartas/Cor-
bis; pp. 17c, 17b Ken Lucas/Visuals Unlimited; pp.
17t, 26t, 38 Daniel Cox/Oxford Scientific Films; pp.
20, 29 John Lemker/Animals Animals; p. 21 Robert
Gill/Corbis; p. 22 Raymond Gehman/Corbis; p. 25
Richard Kolar/Animals Animals; p. 26b Lynn
Stone/Animals Animals; p. 27 R. Planck/Photo
Researchers; p. 28 Ed Wargin/Corbis; p. 30b W. A.
N. T. Photography/Animals Animals; pp. 30t, 31
Ruth Cole/Animals Animals; p. 32 John C. Waugh;
p. 34 Heinemann Library; p. 35 Rick and Nora
Bowers/Visuals Unlimited; p. 36 Theo Allofs/Corbis;
p. 37 Kimberly Saar/Heinemann Library; p. 39b
Gerlach Nature Photography/Animals Animals; p.
39t Ross Frid/Visuals Unlimited; p. 40b Rob and
Ann Simpson/Visuals Unlimited; p. 42 Richard P.
Smith; p. 44b Courtesy of the Michigan Depart-
ment of State, Loon design by the Michigan
Department of Natural Resources ; p. 44t Carmela
Leszczynski/Animals Animals

Cover photographs by (center) Conrad Zobel/Cor-
bis; (top, L-R) David Muench/Corbis, Gerlach
Nature Photography/Animals Animals, Daniel
Cox/Oxford Scientific Film, D. R. Planck/Photo
Researchers

The publisher would like to thank expert reader Lori
A. Martin, research and outreach specialist, Travel,
Tourism, and Recreation Resource Center, Michigan
State University.

Also, special thanks to Alexandra Fix and Bernice
Anne Houseward for their curriculum guidance.

Every effort has been made to contact copyright
holders of any material reproduced in this book.
Any omissions will be rectified in subsequent print-
ings if notice is given to the publisher.

Some words are shown in bold, **like this.**
You can find out what they mean by looking
in the glossary.

Contents

Introduction

Michigan is called the Great Lakes State because it is bordered by four of the five Great Lakes. Only Lake Ontario does not border Michigan. Each of Michigan's Great Lakes help define Michigan as a **peninsula.**

The state of Michigan and the Great Lakes that border it were formed millions of years ago by glaciers. The movement of glaciers created a variety of land formations and **ecosystems** for plants and animals.

Michigan's earliest peoples discovered forests, lakes, and rivers here, as well as beaches and sand dunes. These **habitats** provided **prehistoric** peoples with a wide assortment of wildlife and plant life—everything they needed for food, shelter, and clothing. Later, Native American tribes explored the same **fertile** land. The Ottawa named the land "Michigama," which means "great lake."

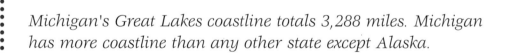

Michigan's Great Lakes coastline totals 3,288 miles. Michigan has more coastline than any other state except Alaska.

By the 1600s, French explorers were paddling through the waters surrounding Michigan. Once these explorers found Michigan's rich **resources,** especially the heavily forested land where many animals lived, they were eager to stay and build trading camps and **missions.** Explorers wanted to trade their European goods for animal **pelts,** especially warm beaver furs that the French used to make hats.

There are about 250,000 acres of sand dunes in Michigan. This is the largest group of freshwater sand dunes in the world.

Word of Michigan's rich forests and connecting lakes and rivers spread to eastern settlements, too. However, while Michigan offered **abundant** forests and thousands of miles of lakeshore, rivers, and **inland** lakes, it was difficult for early settlers to reach easily. This left Michigan out of the westward movement until better roads and canals for transportation were constructed.

*French explorers found plants and animals in Michigan that they had never seen before. Europeans were also responsible for bringing **non-native** plants to Michigan as well.*

By the time Michigan became the 26th state of the United States on January 26, 1837, better transportation brought settlers by the thousands to the area. To these early settlers, Michigan's many **resources** must have seemed endless. Settlers cut down trees so they could live on the land. During Michigan's famous lumber **era,** woodland plant and animal **habitats** decreased or disappeared. As a result, some of the **species** that once **thrived** have become **extinct, endangered,** or **extirpated.** Today, the wildlife, plants, and trees that led the explorers and settlers to Michigan are not as plentiful as they were before. The people and government are working to recreate new local **ecosystems** and preserve what still exists.

Did You Know?

- Michigan has more miles of freshwater shoreline than any other state.
- More than 90 percent of the Upper Peninsula is forested.
- People who live in Michigan are no farther than 6 miles from an **inland** lake, river, or stream, no matter where they live. They are also no farther than 85 miles from a Great Lake.
- Lake Superior is the largest Great Lake and the coldest in water temperature. It is also the deepest (1,332 feet) with an average depth of 500 feet. It is the largest freshwater body of water in the world. Like the other Great Lakes that surround Michigan, Lake Superior has a Native American name that describes it. It is called *kitchi gama* by the Chippewa, pronounced "gitchee gumee." This means "great lake."

Endangered, Extinct, and Extirpated

The three E's are important words in Michigan's natural history because they explain what happened before laws were passed to protect wildlife.

Endangered means that there are very few members of a plant or animal species remaining in an ecosystem. **Conservation** groups work to prevent the endangered species from losing their habitat and to increase their populations. The barn owl and the gray wolf are examples of endangered animals in Michigan.

Extinct plants and animals are those that once lived in an ecosystem, but no longer live there or anywhere else in the world. For example, the passenger pigeon no longer lives in Michigan, nor anywhere else.

Extirpated describes a species that once lived in an ecosystem but disappeared, usually as a result of loss of habitat. However, these plants and animals may live somewhere else, so they are not extinct. The trumpeter swan is a good example of an extirpated animal from Michigan. Before settlement, trumpeter swans lived in the Great Lakes region and in the marshlands of Michigan's Lower Peninsula. Their numbers dropped off because of hunting and loss of their marsh habitat. They disappeared by the late 1800s. Today, after being **reintroduced,** their numbers are increasing and these birds can be found in Michigan's **wetlands** again.

More words of warning: **special concern** and **threatened.**

Some wildlife species, while not endangered, extinct, or extirpated, concern scientists and conservationists. Threatened species are likely to become endangered. These plants and animals are not yet on the endangered list, but they are protected by Michigan law. Plants and animals that are of special concern are being watched and counted. Once they are studied, they may be counted as threatened and may become protected under Michigan law.

Forests

More than half of Michigan's land is forest. Michigan ranks fifth in the nation for the amount of land used for the production of timber. Michigan has about 18.6 million acres of forest. Only Georgia, North Carolina, Alabama, and Oregon have more.

Many trees, shrubs, and other plants prefer specific types of soils and **climates.** These factors determine the growing regions and the various forest locations.

DECIDUOUS TREES

Deciduous trees have leaves that all fall off about the same time. The sugar maple, a popular Michigan tree, is an example of a deciduous tree. It grows in both valleys and uplands and prefers moist soil.

White, black, and red oak trees grow in the vast hardwood forests along Michigan's southern border, where the climate is **temperate** and the soil is dry. Other hardwood trees such as ash, cherry, and hickory are also plentiful. Birch and aspen trees are also deciduous trees.

CONIFEROUS TREES

Conifers, or coniferous trees, are also called evergreens because they have leaves, sometimes called needles, all year. That is

Over half of Michigan's land is covered by forests.

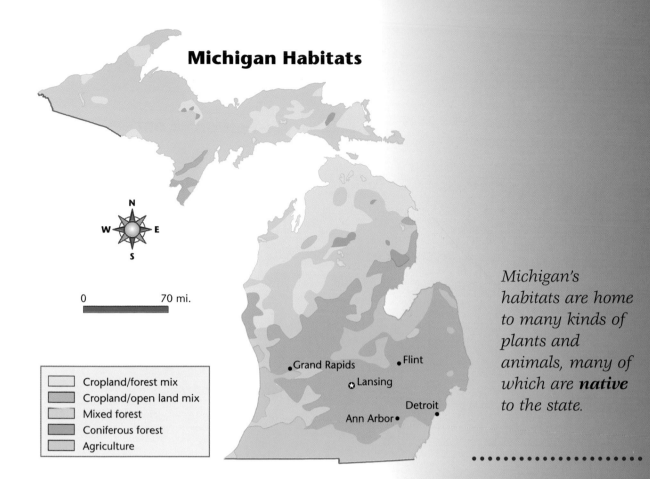

Michigan Habitats

Legend:
- Cropland/forest mix
- Cropland/open land mix
- Mixed forest
- Coniferous forest
- Agriculture

0 ——— 70 mi.

Grand Rapids
Flint
Lansing
Detroit
Ann Arbor

*Michigan's habitats are home to many kinds of plants and animals, many of which are **native** to the state.*

because they grow new leaves throughout the year, not in cycles like deciduous varieties. Conifers also usually have cones that store seeds for new trees.

Huge coniferous softwood forests grow in northern Michigan—pines, firs, and spruce trees. These forests were greatly affected by the lumber **industry,** when many coniferous trees were cut down to provide lumber to build new settlements in Michigan and around the country.

DRAWING THE LINE

Deciduous and coniferous trees grow side by side in the mixed softwood and hardwood forests of the Upper Peninsula. But in the Lower Peninsula, these two types of forests are divided by an imaginary line cutting across Michigan from about Muskegon to Saginaw. Above the line, huge pine trees grow, sometimes five feet in diameter and several hundred feet tall. Below the line, many deciduous trees can be found.

Michigan's state tree, the white pine, is the largest of all of Michigan's coniferous trees.

MICHIGAN FORESTS TODAY

Very few of Michigan's original forests remain. Many of the woodland areas that exist today are due to **preservation** and **reforesting** efforts that began around 1925. Laws needed to be passed before animals, plants, waterfalls, and natural **resources** could be protected from human activities. Building roads to make visiting parks easier and underground mining in and near the parks disturbed animal and plant life. Michigan **legislators** helped the plants and animals by passing laws to protect resources and improve the environment. These laws help natural **habitats** grow.

Laws also help to restore the many natural areas that once covered Michigan. Michigan legislators passed the

Keeping Forests Healthy in Michigan

Michigan's Department of Natural Resources manages many of Michigan's forests. National guidelines help workers measure Michigan's forests by setting some goals and terms. Workers must check on weather conditions, such as storms and droughts, to see how they affect life in the forest. They also measure the **biodiversity** of the forest. Other factors they measure are how large the trees are and how many acres of forestland exist.

Michigan's Original Forests

In the Upper Peninsula, northern hardwood and pine forests in the Hiawatha National Forest in Rapid River, The Porcupines Mountains Wilderness State Park in Ontonagon, and Fort Wilkins State Park in Copper Harbor all still contain some of the original "old growth" trees from the 1800s.

Hartwick Pines State Park in Grayling and Sleeping Bear Dunes National Lakeshore near Empire in the northern Lower Peninsula have examples of original hardwood and pine trees. In the southern Lower Peninsula, original beech and sugar maple trees can be found. These forests still maintain examples from the past, but to preserve them, visitors need to be especially careful while hiking or walking in these parks.

Wilderness and Natural Areas Act in 1972 to dedicate and rename many parks. Today, over 18 million acres, about half of Michigan's total land, is forest. Often these forests are managed and controlled by forest agencies so that young and older growth forests can be kept in balance.

WHITE-TAILED DEER

The white-tailed deer, Michigan's official state **mammal,** can be found in every county in the state as well as in many different habitats, but the forest offers the most protection. Before European settlement in the 1700s, deer herds lived in the Lower Peninsula, where forest habitat was available. When the white-tailed deer habitat decreased because of clearing the land for settlement and farming, the deer began to search for new habitats, including in the Upper Peninsula. To keep warm in winter, deer like thick forests where the leaves of either deciduous trees or coniferous needles provide a natural blanket and protection. Tall grasses that dry in the fall also provide warmth.

Black bears have good eyesight, sharp hearing, and a keen sense of smell.

BLACK BEARS

Michigan's black bears also live in a forest **habitat.** They are the smallest of the bears living in North America, usually weighing between 200 and 300 pounds. They are fast runners and quick tree climbers.

Black bears like to live in hollowed-out logs, dead trees, or underground dens. About 15,000 to 19,000 black bears live in Michigan. Of these bears, nine out of ten live in the Upper Peninsula. However, as more people move into the Upper Peninsula and crowd those habitats, some bears are moving into the northern Lower Peninsula.

WOODPECKERS

Michigan is home to eight **species** of woodpeckers. Two of the most common are the downy woodpecker and the hairy woodpecker. These birds find food in dead trees. They remove the bark from the trees to find insects living there. Woodpeckers also use these trees to nest.

Both downy and hairy woodpeckers are black and white. If the bird's bill is as long as its head, it is a hairy woodpecker. A bird with a bill shorter than the length of its head is a downy woodpecker.

Kirtland's Warbler

In the 1970s, the Kirtland's warbler was placed on the **endangered** species list. The Michigan Department of Natural Resources joined with other groups to provide new forests of jack pine trees where Kirtland's warblers could nest and **breed.** These birds **migrate** to Michigan to breed on the cool forest ground underneath the jack pine trees. Because of these new-growth forests, the Kirtland's warbler's population is growing in Michigan.

White Trillium

In early spring, wildflowers begin to bloom within the forest. One of these flowers is the white trillium. The white trillium has three flower petals. Its name comes from the Latin word for three. Trillium plants are protected by Michigan's Christmas Greens and Wildflower Protection Law of 1962. This law prevents

Only male Kirtland's warblers sing. They can be heard over one-quarter of a mile away!

Many wildflowers need as many as seven years before they store enough food in their roots to produce a flower.

the beautiful flowers of Michigan from becoming **threatened** by limiting their sale and making it illegal to collect these plants if they grow on another person's property. Other forest wildflowers include jack-in-the-pulpit, skunk cabbage, wild garlic, bloodroot, hepatica, Dutchman's breeches, and trout lily. White Canadian violets and blue spiderwort add more color in the forest.

A Food Web

The forest **ecosystem** includes plants, trees, and many kinds of animals who make their homes in Michigan's forests. The way they all relate to each other and depend upon each other for energy and nourishment is called a food chain. The relationship between all plants and animals in one ecosystem is called a food web.

Every food web begins with the sun. The sun provides energy for all living things. Green plants such as grass change the sun's energy, nutrients from soil, and water into food. Plant-eaters, such as mice, eat grass and change it into stored energy in animal tissue.

Meat-eaters, such as hawks, eat mice and transfer the energy again. When animals at the top of the food chain die, decomposers change the animal's tissue back into nutrients that plants can use to make food.

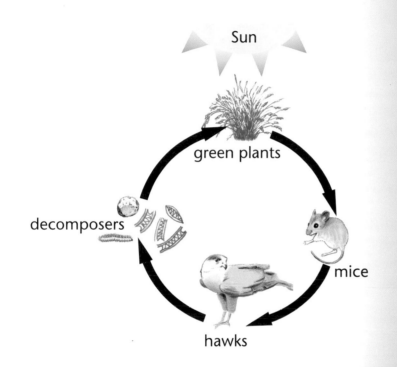

Sun

green plants

decomposers

mice

hawks

Non-Native Plants

Since settlers arrived, about 800 **non-native** plant **species** have also come to Michigan. Some were **introduced** by accident. Seeds may have been carried into Michigan by birds and other animals. Other plants were brought from Europe and other **continents** and planted in Michigan.

The way non-native plants came is not as important as how they get along with the **native** plants. Many non-native plants crowd out and take over the **habitat** of Michigan's native plants that have been growing for thousands of years. Non-native plants prevent the healthy native habitats from surviving.

The Great Lakes, Sand Dunes, and Beaches

The waters of the Great Lakes and the sands that surround them provide **ecosystems** for Michigan's plants and animals. The five Great Lakes contain about one-fifth of the world's fresh surface water supply. People living in both the United States and Canada depend on the lakes for drinking water, food, recreation, and transportation.

The fish found in the Great Lakes consist of both **native** and **introduced species.** Common catches include lake trout, salmon, walleye, perch, white fish, smallmouth bass, steelhead, and brown trout.

Some lake trout live to be over 25 years old.

LAKE TROUT

Lake trout are the third-most important fish caught **commercially** in the Great Lakes. They are greenish-gray in color, and are found in deep, cool lakes. Lake trout eat insects, small fish, fish eggs, and shellfish. These fish are also called Mackinaw trout, Great Lakes trout, and salmon trout.

SALMON

Most people think of salmon as an ocean fish, but it also lives in the fresh waters of the Great Lakes because it has been **stocked.** Atlantic salmon are stocked in Lake Ontario, and chinook and coho salmon are stocked in all five Great Lakes. These fish need to be restocked each year because they have not been successful enough in reproducing on their own to keep their population steady. Chinook salmon are one of Lake Michigan's most prized **game** fish.

*Salmon make a difficult journey home to **spawn.***

WALLEYE

Walleye were a popular commercial fish in the 1940s and 1950s. Today, sport fishers enjoy catching the small fish. Walleye range from 13 to 25 inches in length and 1 to 5 pounds in weight. They can live for up to 7 years, but are generally caught when they are between 1 and 3 years old.

Walleye are the largest members of the perch family.

YELLOW PERCH

One of the most plentiful fish in Lakes Superior, Michigan, and Huron is the yellow perch. The yellow perch is usually smaller than common perch, weighing less than 1 pound. It swims in **schools** and mainly eats meat, such as insects and other smaller fish.

Yellow perch are the most frequently caught game fish in Michigan.

WHITEFISH

As the most important **commercial** fish in Lakes Ontario and Huron, whitefish catches can bring in as much as $5 million a year. Whitefish are also an important part of Lake Michigan commercial fishing, and a popular **game** fish in all of the Great Lakes.

SMALLMOUTH BASS

Smallmouth bass are known by several names, including northern smallmouth bass, black bass, brown bass, and white or mountain trout. These fish can grow to be 15 to 20 inches and 2 pounds in weight. They prefer darkness and waters above 50 degrees. Smallmouth bass eat insects, crayfish, and other small fish. Popular with fishers, smallmouth bass are known to put up a good fight when caught on a fishing line.

STEELHEAD

Steelhead is the name given to rainbow trout that live in the Great Lakes. Steelheads are not **native** to the Great Lakes. They were **introduced** to these waters because they are popular with fishers. Steelheads eat plankton, minnows, insects, and sometimes small fish. They can grow to be 36 inches long and weigh 20 pounds, but most steelhead living in the Great Lakes only grow to be 16 inches and 8 to 9 pounds.

Fishing for Money

Approximately 2 million Michigan residents and 334,000 nonresident tourists fish in Michigan each year. This brings in over $1.4 billion each year and provides over 18,000 jobs.

BROWN TROUT

Brown trout weigh 2 to 8 pounds and reach a length of up to 24 inches. They are light brown in color, with silvery sides and bellies. Brown trout feed at night, so fishers are

*Michigan's dunes support a wide variety of **habitats.** The dunes are also home to five **threatened** and **endangered species.***

their most dangerous enemies. Because of this, brown trout tend to live longer than most other fish.

SAND DUNES

Sand dunes are formed when wind or water sweep sand into piles on land. Plant life helps to protect the dunes and keep them in place as the sand dries. Sand dunes have different shapes and heights, depending upon the conditions. The sand that collects in the dunes is used in **industry.** Michigan is one of the country's top dune sand producers and supplies the dune sand used to mine oil and in the manufacture of glass and fiberglass.

Lake Michigan has the largest amount of freshwater sand dunes in the world. Dunes begin at the edge of the lake as just sand. As you move further away from the water, grasses grow. A little further in, forests appear.

Many people mistakenly blame goldenrod for causing allergies. The goldenrod flowers bloom at the same time as ragweed, which does not have pretty flowers. It is the ragweed that causes itching and sneezing.

PLANT LIFE

Plant life along the sand dunes has adapted to the summertime dry, hot, windy conditions and lake temperatures. The tall dune grass survives because of its deep roots that can absorb ground water. Other plants, like the sea rocket, have leaves that absorb and hold moisture. Many spring wildflowers, such as the dune lily and Pitcher's thistle, decorate the dunes. Trillium, jack-in-the-pulpit, cone flowers, asters, and goldenrods also all bloom within Michigan's dune **ecosystem.**

HOUGHTON'S GOLDENROD

Houghton's goldenrod is found only along Lakes Michigan and Huron. It lives among the dunes to prevent sand **erosion.** This plant typically grows on moist sandy beaches. It is threatened by human traffic, both on foot and in cars.

BEACH PEA

One of the flowering plants that helps protect the sand dunes is the beach pea. It has small blue-purple flowers and blooms in the summer. It grows close to the ground and has underground stems that connect the plants. The beach pea's small, thick leaves keep the sand in place.

MARRAM GRASS

Marram grass is one of the most important plants in the dune **habitat** because it helps keep the sand from blowing away. Its stems grow on the ground to protect the shifting sand. Marram grass has short roots and coarse, stiff stems.

One of the unique qualities of marram grass is that it likes to be buried. As sand grains cover the marram grass, it grows high to make its way above the sand.

LAKE HURON TANSY

This **threatened** plant, with yellow leaves and long stems, lives near the northern shore of Lake Michigan, and on the shores of Lake Huron and Lake Superior. It was used as a medicine long ago, but it is now known to be poisonous. The Lake Huron Tansy has lacy, hairy leaves and a yellow flower head that blooms in the mid- to late summer.

BIRDS

Hundreds of birds make their homes, for at least part of the year, near the dunes, beaches, and Great Lakes bordering Michigan. Birds that live in Michigan year-round are called residents. They are called **migrants** if they live in Michigan only part of the year.

Raccoons are just some of the animals that make their homes in sand dunes. These animals find food and shelter in their sandy surroundings.

One of the **migrants** is the heron. It is often seen standing perfectly still at the water's edge. That is how it fishes. When it spots a fish, it quickly jabs it with its long beak. Herons nest in trees. When many herons build nests in the same tree or close together, it is called a heronry.

ANIMAL WILDLIFE

Many animal **species** make their **habitats** in the dune **ecosystem,** too. A few of the animals that live among the dunes and the dune plant life include the mink, muskrat, fox, and squirrel. The red fox and coyote also live in the dune forest habitat. The red fox is **nocturnal.** It lives throughout Michigan, especially in the coastal dunes where it can easily find food such as mice, birds, insects, plants, and berries. Snakes and turtles, as well as toads and salamanders, also live in the dunes.

TREES OF THE DUNE FOREST

Although a long strip of sand dunes reaching 200 feet high are the most widely known feature of the Michigan lakeshore, the forest on the edge of the dunes is also unique. Thanks to dune plants that protect the dunes from **erosion,** forests actually grow near the open dunes. Trees that make up the various dune forests include ash, maple, pine, hemlock, and cottonwood.

*Wind moves sand **inland** away from the lake. Trees near sand dunes prevent the sand from creeping further and further away from shore.*

Inland Lakes, Rivers, and Streams

The glaciers of **prehistoric** times created most of Michigan's **inland** waterways as well as all of the Great Lakes. The melting glacial ice filled the deep grooves left by the glaciers as they slowly moved across the land several times over millions of years.

Michigan rivers are unique because many of them, especially those blocked by sand dunes bordering Lake Michigan, flow into smaller lakes before entering a Great Lake. Eventually, all of Michigan's river water reaches Lakes Michigan, Huron, Superior, or Erie. Because of this, many of the same fish that live in the Great Lakes also live in Michigan's inland lakes, rivers, and streams.

Michigan has over 36,000 miles of streams, and more than 11,000 lakes and ponds.

There are many types of plants and animals that **thrive** in wet environments. The Great Lakes, Michigan's many lakes, rivers, and streams, and its coastlines provide a unique **habitat** for many plants and animals.

PAINTED TURTLE

The painted turtle, Michigan's official state reptile, has yellow and red stripes on its head, and red stripes on its tail and legs. It can live in other habitats, but wet areas provide year-round conditions for **breeding,** feeding, and **hibernating** in the muddy bottom of streams and lakes. Turtles eat plants and small animals. Because **wetlands,** lakes, and streams are decreasing in Michigan, state laws protect Michigan's turtles from **extinction.**

GREAT BLUE HERON

The great blue heron is one of the many birds that can be found nesting and feeding along the shores of Michigan's

A group of fifth-graders from Brandywine Elementary School in Niles asked the Michigan state government to declare the painted turtle the state reptile in 1995.

Because of disappearing habitats, only one in five heron hatchlings survive.

lakes and streams. This bird builds its nest in hardwood trees. It feeds on fish and other small animals it catches with its long beak, such as frogs, salamanders, and snakes.

SANDHILL CRANE

The sandhill crane is another Michigan shore bird found in both the Upper and Lower Peninsulas. Larger than the great blue heron, its **habitats** decreased when humans interfered with it. About 800 pairs of cranes have been counted in Michigan recently. Cranes eat both plants and small animals such as snails, crayfish, and mice. Cranes also eat plant nuts, such as acorns, seeds, and berries. Sometimes cranes will even eat grains and seeds found on farms.

COMMON LOON

One of Michigan's **threatened species** is the common loon. It has a black head, a pointed bill, and a white chest. The loon builds its nest along the shore of Michigan's shallow streams and **inland** lakes. It catches fish by looking beneath the water and then diving below the surface.

A loon's feet are at the back of its body instead of underneath. Loons walk with the help of their wings and beak and cannot take off from land.

DUCKWEED

Duckweed is the tiniest known flowering plant and is common throughout Michigan. It floats on top of ponds and streams and gets its name because it is eaten by ducks and fish. Duckweed has many uses. Scientists are using duckweed **clones** and **genes** to produce medicines. Others are using duckweed to remove pollutants from water.

Duckweed is often confused with algae, or thought to be "slime." Duckweed is actually good for the water, as it removes harmful substances and provides food for animals there.

CATTAILS

These tall, slender plants live in **wetlands** and at the edge of rivers and streams in Michigan. Cattails produce thousands of tiny brown flowers on the end of its long stem. Cattails can grow as high as nine feet tall. They are commonly found around the edge of wetlands, lakes, and ponds. Birds and fish use cattails for hiding.

Swamps, Marshes, and Wetlands

Michigan has another type of watery **habitat** called **wetlands.** Shallow bodies of water or soil that contain a large amount of water are considered wetlands. There are four main types of wetlands. Marshes are usually associated with ponds, lakes, or streams. Typical marsh plants include rushes, sedges, cattails, and lily pads. Swamps are wetlands found in forests with conifers, hardwoods, and other forest plants. Bogs are areas with very little water flow, **peat** soils, and many mosses. Black spruce, blueberries, cranberries, orchids, and

Wetlands are places of great beauty. They offer opportunities for hiking, canoeing, birdwatching, and fishing.

insect-eating plants are also found here. Fens are similar to bogs but with better soil because of more water flowing through. In fens, sedges and low shrubs are widespread, along with some orchids and insect-eating plants.

Wetlands provide habitats for many kinds of plants and animals. Wetland animals include muskrats, beavers, ducks, geese, plovers, sandpipers, herons, rails, salamanders, frogs, toads, dragonflies, and mayflies. For ducks, geese, and other **migratory** birds, wetlands are the most important part of the migratory cycle. Wetlands provide food and a safe habitat. Many **species** of Great Lakes fish also depend on coastal wetlands for successful reproduction.

PURPLE LOOSESTRIFE

Purple loosestrife is a **non-native** plant. Because it crowds out **native** plants that would normally grow in the wetlands, it affects the plant **diversity.** It also affects the animal habitat because it crowds out plants that the animals normally eat. Purple loosestrife has been found in every county in the southern Lower Peninsula, and throughout the northern Lower Peninsula and Upper

Some Michigan students take part in the Purple Loosestrife Project. They learn how this plant affects the environment and safe ways to control the plant's growth.

Muskrats live in or near water most of their lives. Their fur is nearly waterproof. It keeps the muskrats warm and dry, even in the winter when the water freezes.

Peninsula as well. It was brought by European settlers who used the plant as an herbal medicine.

MUSKRAT

The muskrat gets its name from its musk-like smell. It has webbed back feet that help it paddle through the water. It can stay underwater for up to 20 minutes at a time. It feeds on plant roots and stalks found near and in the water, as well as small water animals and small birds. Muskrats also live in rivers and lakes.

BEAVER

Beavers prefer the surroundings of a wet environment. The furry, flat tailed beaver lives in **wetland habitats** as well as in rivers and lakes. It spends its time building dams and lodges, another word for the beaver's home. It uses its large front teeth to strip bark off branches and to cut through tree trunks. The lodges are often large enough for several beaver families and have underwater tunnels and entrances.

AMPHIBIANS

A vernal pool is unique type of wetland found in forests. This term describes a small pool that forms after the winter thaw and attracts amphibians to lay eggs there. By summertime, after

Michigan is home to eleven species of frogs and two species of toads.

the young have developed into adult frogs, salamanders, and toads, the vernal pools dry up. Michigan amphibians depend on the wetlands to **breed.** Michigan has 13 **species** of frogs and toads, and 10 species of salamanders.

BLUE-SPOTTED SALAMANDER

Salamanders are amphibians. Several salamander species call Michigan home, but the blue-spotted salamander is among the most common. It usually has bluish-turquoise spots on its body, but it sometimes looks gray without spots. It lives under rotting logs in hardwood marshes. It also lives in moist conditions where it can find insects, worms, spiders, and other small animals for food. The salamander has several ways of protecting itself

Salamanders are very secretive. They prefer to stay away from human activity, and only come out at night.

from **predators** such as fish, snakes, and raccoons. The blue-spotted salamander has a scent gland that releases an offensive and sometimes poisonous chemical. Its skin becomes slimy and slippery so it can not be easily caught. If a predator gets too close to it, the blue-spotted salamander wiggles its tail until it falls off. While the hungry predator is wrestling with the wriggling tail, the salamander escapes. The salamander's tail grows back over time.

SHRINKING WETLANDS

In the last 100 years, half of Michigan's wetlands have disappeared. Some of the causes are pollution and construction, logging and mining, and draining and **dredging** of the wetland areas. Bogs are more common

Wetlands Preservation Act

In 1979, Michigan passed a state law to protect its wetlands. This law requires landowners to apply for a permit from the state in order to **dredge,** fill, drain, or construct in wetlands. The person applying for the permit must prove that they have done everything possible to not harm the wetland. The Department of Environmental Quality must approve the permit before the activity can begin.

in the Upper Peninsula because many **wetlands** areas in the southern portion of the Lower Peninsula have been drained. The water is removed and the soil is dried enough for planting. Crops such as celery, radishes, lettuce, and mint are commonly grown on Michigan's muck farms, the term given to farming in areas that have been changed from wetlands. The rich black soil is good for farming for the same reasons it is important to the animals and plants that live in the wetlands. Sometimes the soil is taken off the wetlands and sold as top soil.

Nature preserves and parks in Michigan have wetlands that are being saved from destruction. A few of these protected areas include Saul Lake Bog Nature Preserve in Kent County and Kal-Haven Trail, a state park that crosses wetland areas between Kalamazoo and South Haven in the southern Lower Peninsula.

Along the length of the Kal-Haven Trail are seven bridges that cross valleys, streams, and wetlands.

Extinct Animals

Michigan's earliest animals lived millions of years ago. Michigan's fossil record shows that some of the largest **prehistoric carnivores** lived in the area. Many people think of dinosaurs when they are asked to name large **extinct** animals, but scientists have found evidence of other prehistoric animals as well.

WHALES

Scientists learned that whales once lived in what is now Michigan. Whale bones and teeth from three different whale **species**—finback whales, sperm whales, and right whales—have been discovered in Michigan's Lower Peninsula. Whales usually live in deep oceans, so scientists can only guess how these prehistoric whales reached Michigan. Some think whales may have arrived long ago when Michigan was covered by a deep sea.

MASTODONS

Mastodons looked like large elephants with long curved tusks. They lived in Michigan more than 10,000 years ago. Mastodon bones have been found at various locations around the state. Mastodons ate from fir and spruce trees. They disappeared as the **climate** warmed and their food became scarce. They were also hunted by Paleo-Indians.

Mastodons were named the Michigan state fossil in 2002.

WOOLLY MAMMOTHS

Woolly mammoths are an **extinct** plant-eating **mammal** that stand about ten feet tall. They had a large bump on top of their heads and coarse, thick fur that kept them warm during the cold Pleistocene **Era,** which occurred from about 1.6 million years ago to 11,000 years ago.

GIANT BEAVERS

Paleontologists discovered that the giant beaver was about the same size as black bears that lived in Michigan. Beavers lived during the most recent **prehistoric** time period known as the Pleistocene Era. These large rodents disappeared, becoming another of Michigan's extinct **species.**

PETOSKEY STONE

Michigan's most famous fossil is the Petoskey stone. This fossil shows that **invertebrates** lived here 245 to 570 million years ago. Most fossils are rare, but the Petoskey stone can be found quite easily near the city of Petoskey, where rocks remain in layers of Alpena limestone. The stones can also be found along the Lake Michigan and Lake Huron beaches in the Lower Peninsula during spring and summer. The Petoskey stone shows the fossilized six-sided *Hexagonaria* species of coral. The special coral makes a honeycomb design on a Petoskey stone.

The Petoskey stone became the official state stone in 1965. The name Petoskey is a version of the name Petosegay. It means "rising sun" or "rays of dawn."

It is thought that the Carolina parakeet was as smart as chimpanzees and dolphins.

CAROLINA PARAKEET

During the mid-1800s, millions of these brightly colored green birds with yellow heads were killed so their feathers could be used to decorate women's hats. They were also caught and caged as pets. They did not sing or "talk," but they were pretty and could recognize their names. By 1920, these beautiful birds were extinct.

BLUE PIKE

The blue pike is perhaps the most recent Michigan species to become extinct. This fish lived only in the Great Lakes region and became extinct in 1970. Several factors led to its extinction. One, it was over-fished by sport fishing and the fishing **industry.** One estimate is that a billion pounds of blue pike was caught between 1885 and the early 1960s. Another reason for its extinction came from the settlement of Michigan and the other states bordering Lake Erie and Lake Ontario, where most of the blue pike lived. As settlement increased, the natural fish **habitat** of clear, cool water was disturbed. People and industry destroyed the **wetlands, introduced non-native** fish species into the Great Lakes, and caused water pollution. Three other Great Lakes fish—the longjaw cisco, deepwater cisco, and the blackfin cisco—also disappeared.

Endangered Plants and Animals

Michigan's forests, **wetlands,** and **prairies** nearly disappeared after large numbers of European settlers arrived in the 1800s. Better transportation brought more and more settlers, and towns grew into major cities. Not only did settlers need the land for living space, new **industries,** such as Michigan's timber industry, were necessary to build cities and to fuel factories. All this growth changed Michigan's natural areas.

Bald eagles living near water signal that the water is of good quality.

What effect did this have on the wildlife **habitats** in these **ecosystems?** Some plants and animals disappeared when their habitat changed or was destroyed. If they left Michigan in search of a new habitat, perhaps in another state, they are considered **extirpated.** When an animal's population and habitats decrease and **conservationists** fear it might become **extinct,** it becomes **endangered.** Endangered **species** are protected by law. Sometimes wildlife is not yet at the endangered stage, but is in danger of becoming endangered. They are considered **threatened.** Another group of plants and animals are placed on a **special concern** list. They are species that are being counted and watched because scientists believe their numbers may be decreasing.

Michigan Wildlife Refuges

Lake Superior
Huron
Marquette
Whitefish Point
Pendills Creek
Hiawatha Forest
Seney
Harbor Island
Ironwood
Iron Mountain
Mackinaw City
Cheboygan
Gravel Island
Michigan Island
Jordan River
Alpena
Michigan Island
Lake Huron
Muskegon River
Kirtland's Warbler
Bay City
Shiawassee
Grand River
Lansing
Lake Michigan
Kalamazoo River
Ann Arbor
Detroit
Detroit River International Wildlife Refuge
Paw Paw River
Huron River
St. Joseph River
Lake Erie

National Wildlife Refuge
National Fish Hatchery

0 — 70 mi.

N W E S

Michigan's wildlife refuges offer opportunities for bird watching, viewing wildlife, nature study, hiking, mountain biking, canoeing, freshwater fishing, hunting, viewing historical sights, nature photography, scenic driving, and more.

The eastern portion of the Upper Peninsula is bordered by Lakes Michigan, Huron, and Superior. Forests in this region are home to many of Michigan's endangered or threatened animals, including the bald eagle, the gray wolf, and the piping plover. The Michigan monkey-flower and dwarf lake iris are two of Michigan's protected plants from this region.

BALD EAGLE

Perhaps the most well-known of all endangered species is the bald eagle. It became the official symbol of the United States in 1872, but settlement and loss of habitat, as well as deliberate killing by those who thought the eagle was a pest, nearly caused its extinction both in Michigan and across the United States. The bald eagle is a bird of **prey,** at the top of its food chain. After settlement caused habitat changes for smaller birds who lived along Michigan's lakeshores, the eagle had less food. Some of its food became **contaminated** by harmful chemicals and pesticides. Bald eagles, in turn, were killed when they ate infected **species** below them on the food chain. They were placed on the **endangered** list in 1979.

In 2003, Michigan's Department of Natural Resources reported an increase in the number of bald eagles in Michigan. Bird counters recorded more than 1,200 bald eagles in the southern portion of the Lower Peninsula. The count in 2002 was only 324. Improving the environment contributes to the higher count. Limiting the use of harmful pesticides and decreasing the dumping of toxic **industrial** waste into waterways are two ways to improve the environment and reduce the causes of birth defects and death in animals. When more animals survive, the food chain becomes stronger.

Gray wolves are also known as timber wolves and eastern timber wolves. They are related to coyotes and red and gray foxes.

GRAY WOLF

The gray wolf, also known as the timber wolf, lived in large numbers throughout Michigan before settlers arrived. They were animals of **prey.** They hunted moose, bison, elk, and other animals, but these animals, like the gray wolf, lost their **habitat** once human settlement began. To survive, gray wolves preyed on other animals for food, such as farmers' sheep and cattle. By the early 1900s, wolves became endangered and were considered a dangerous enemy to farmers. In 1965, Michigan began protecting the gray wolf, but it was not recognized by the federal government until the passage of the Endangered Species Act of 1973.

Conservation programs worked to **reintroduce** the gray wolf in Michigan and elsewhere in the United States. In Michigan, the gray wolf population has grown from about 20 in 1992 to more than 275 in 2002. Today, packs of gray wolves prey on deer, rodents, and other small animals, but they also eat nuts and berries. They live in large forests, mostly in the Upper Peninsula. Because people of Michigan accept the gray wolf as part of Michigan's natural animal life and have approved their recovery programs, the gray wolf's classification has changed to **threatened.**

MICHIGAN MONKEY-FLOWER

The Michigan monkey-flower is a plant that grows in only 12 places in Michigan. Its habitat was once found in **wetlands** near lakeshores. As development increased, these natural areas were drained. The Michigan monkey-flower cannot survive without spring flows of melting snow and ice. They became endangered when their unique habitat changed.

Explorers Lewis and Clark first found the monkey-flower in Montana. This plant no longer lives outside of Michigan.

DWARF LAKE IRIS

The dwarf lake iris gets its name from its tiny flowers that are about the size of a quarter. They are usually bright blue, but can also be white or purple. The dwarf lake iris only grows near the shores and behind the dunes of Lake Huron and Lake Michigan. Its habitat has changed for several reasons. Dune buggies and other off-road vehicles have damaged its habitat. Development of shorefront property, chemical insecticides, and people picking the tiny flowers are other reasons this Michigan plant has decreased.

The dwarf lake iris is Michigan's state wildflower.

Michigan runs a Piping Plover Patrol during the summer months. Volunteers talk with beach or park visitors, making them aware that the piping plover is nesting and point out closed areas of the beach or park.

PIPING PLOVER

This small **endangered** bird lives along the shores of Lake Michigan during warm months and **migrates** to the Gulf of Mexico and southern Atlantic coasts during the winter. It eats insect larvae and small marine animals it finds in the dunes and along the beach. It builds its nest on the ground where the female usually lays four eggs. The eggs are **camouflaged** to look like small pebbles. The piping plover became nearly **extinct** after its **habitat**—beaches and dunes—became favorite recreational areas for humans.

STURGEON

The largest freshwater fish is the sturgeon. It is believed that sturgeon began living in the Great Lakes 400 million years ago during the Devonian **Era.** This amazing fish can live for 100 years and weigh up to 150 pounds. Sturgeon eat zebra mussels. Instead of having scales, they are covered by rows of bony plates. Sturgeon are endangered and protected by law.

Michigan and Wisconsin are home to the last large populations of sturgeon.

MITCHELL'S SATYR BUTTERFLY

This endangered butterfly is found only in 13 places in Michigan and 2 in Indiana. It lives in **wetland** fens. The butterfly has become endangered because of habitat destruction, pollution, and over-collection by butterfly collectors.

Endangered and Extinct Animals

Michigan has a long list of endangered animals, as well as a "special" list of plants and animals that are being watched because of reducing numbers. A few of the **species** are listed here:

Endangered in Michigan

Redside dace	Smallmouth salamander	Barn owl
Creek chubsucker	Kirtland's snake	Cougar
Silver shiner	Short-eared owl	Lynx
Northern madtom	Piping plover	Prairie vole
Pugnose minnow	Prairie warbler	Indiana bat
River darter	Kirtland's warbler	Migrant loggerhead
Channel darter	Peregrine falcon	shrike
Southern redbelly dace	King rail	

Threatened in Michigan

Lake sturgeon	Spotted turtle	Least bittern
Eastern sand darter	Henslow's sparrow	Osprey
Cisco or lake herring	Long-eared owl	Caspian tern
Shortjaw cisco	Red-shouldered hawk	Common tern
Mooneye	Yellow rail	Trumpeter tern
River redhorse	Yellow-throated warbler	Gray wolf
Sauger	Merlin	Least shrew
Marbled salamander	Common loon	
Eastern fox snake	Bald eagle	

People, Plants, and Animals

Humans have been changing Michigan's **ecosystems** since they first arrived in Michigan. However, humans have found ways to make positive changes. In recent years, successful Michigan **conservation** programs have worked to rebuild some of the natural **habitats** that were lost. Laws protect **endangered** and **threatened species,** and plants and animals are being **reintroduced** once their habitats are restored.

There is one ecosystem that is often overlooked because it is not a distinctive forest, **wetland,** river, dune, or lake. Wildlife also lives and grows in cities and towns. These are called **urban** areas. Because urban areas have replaced many Michigan forest habitats, plants and animals have adapted to survive in those areas where people live, work, and play. People can and do help create habitats, making it easier for plants and animals to survive. Sometimes it just happens by accident.

Raccoons are not shy when it comes to getting food!

ANIMALS IN THE CITY

One of Michigan's endangered species, the peregrine falcon, lives in Detroit and Grand Rapids on high stone ledges of buildings, overlooking the busy cities. To the peregrine falcon, skyscrapers are similar to the stone cliffs of its usual habitat. It finds pigeons and other small birds for food. City living keeps **predators,** such as the great horned owl, from finding it.

Other animals, like the gray squirrel, live in large trees in city neighborhoods just like they do in the wild. Mice are also common in cities and neighborhoods. They eat human food and garbage. The raccoon is a clever **scavenger,** eating its way into garbage bins and removing lids that are not securely fastened. Woodchucks and chipmunks live underground in tunnels. They build more than one entrance to help them escape from predators.

Many Squirrels

Michigan is the only state in the U.S. that is home to six species of squirrels. The red, black, and eastern gray squirrels can be found in both the Upper and Lower Peninsula, but the southern flying and eastern fox live only in the Lower Peninsula. The northern flying squirrel can be found in the northern Lower Peninsula and entire Upper Peninsula.

BACKYARD HABITATS

To create backyards that attract wildlife, it is important to understand plant and animal requirements. The basic needs of wildlife are water, food, protection from the **climate** and predators, and space.

For example, white-tailed deer eat the unique needles of white pine trees. Deer also prefer white cedar and maple

*Raccoons will make a home anywhere that is safe from **predators,** which includes humans.*

trees over other types of trees. Although backyards are not forests, a neighborhood planted with many trees and **native** plants may look like a forest to hungry deer.

Some neighborhoods have small creeks and streams running through them. These natural **wetland habitats** can be maintained by keeping them free of pollution. Using pesticides that eventually run into streams destroys habitats for plants and animals. Planting **seedlings** along the banks provides habitats and food for area wildlife. A **buffer** zone of trees also prevents **erosion** and helps prevent pollution from reaching the stream.

LENDING NATURE A HAND

Human awareness about safeguarding nature is working in school and community programs. Special interest license plates attract attention to nature's needs, and state symbols often represent **threatened** or **endangered species.** Private citizens, state agencies, and wildlife associations work to protect and increase Michigan's **ecosystems.** In recent years, wildlife that was listed as endangered or threatened has been **reintroduced** because of these efforts.

Michigan residents can purchase a special license plate for their cars. The money raised from these plates helps protect Michigan's wildlife.

Map of Michigan

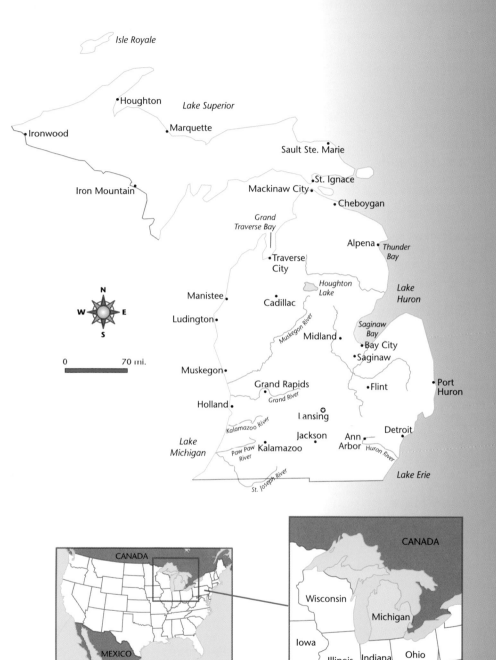

Isle Royale

Houghton

Lake Superior

Marquette

Ironwood

Sault Ste. Marie

Iron Mountain

St. Ignace

Mackinaw City

Cheboygan

Grand Traverse Bay

Alpena

Thunder Bay

Traverse City

Houghton Lake

Lake Huron

Manistee

Cadillac

Ludington

Saginaw Bay

Midland

Bay City

Muskegon River

Saginaw

Muskegon

Grand Rapids

Flint

Port Huron

Grand River

Holland

Lansing

Kalamazoo River

Detroit

Paw Paw River

Kalamazoo

Jackson

Ann Arbor

Lake Michigan

Huron River

Lake Erie

St. Joseph River

N
W   E
S

0   70 mi.

CANADA

MEXICO

CANADA

Wisconsin

Michigan

Iowa

Illinois   Indiana   Ohio

Glossary

abundant large quantity

biodiversity biological variety in an environment as shown by the number of different kinds of plants and animals

breed to produce offspring

buffer something that serves as a protective barrier

camouflage blending in with surroundings to hide

carnivore meat-eater

climate weather conditions that are usual for a certain area

clone exact copy

commercial product that is bought and sold

conservation planned management of natural resources to prevent waste, destruction, or neglect. People who work to conserve the environment are called conservationists.

contaminate make unclean

continent one of the great divisions of land on the globe; Asia, Antarctica, Australia, Africa, Europe, North America, and South America are the seven continents of the world

diversity having variety

dredge dig into the bottom of a body of water

ecosystem community of living things, together with the environment in which they live

endanger threatened with extinction

era historical period of time

erosion wearing away by high winds or rushing water

extirpate move from the place a plant or animal once was, like to another state

extinct no longer living

fertile bearing crops or vegetation in abundance

game animal hunted for food or sport

gene unit of DNA that controls the development of an organism

habitat place where an animal or plant lives and grows

hibernating passing through the winter in a resting state

industry group of businesses that offer a similar product or service

inland not near the coast

introduce bring something to a place where it has not been before

invertebrate animal without a backbone

legislator member of the governmental body that makes laws

mammal warm-blooded animal with a backbone; female mammals produce milk for feeding their young

migrant something that moves from place to place, usually on a regular schedule

migrate to move from one place to another for food or to breed

mission small town based around a church

native originally from a certain area

nocturnal active at night

non-native not originally from the area

paleontologist scientist who studies fossils

peat dry, lightweight, spongy substance that forms when dead plants break down under certain conditions

pelt animal fur

peninsula piece of land that is surrounded by water on three sides

prairie large area of grassland

predator animal that lives mostly by killing and eating other animals

prehistoric from the time before history was written

preservation keeping from injury, loss, or decay

prey animal hunted or killed by another animal for food

reforesting renewing forest growth by planting new trees

reintroduce bring something back to the place it once was

resource something that is available to take care of a need; there are natural and human-made resources

scavenger animal that searches through junk and garbage to find food

school large number of one kind of fish swimming together

seedling young plant that is grown from seed

spawn lay eggs

special concern species of plants or animals that scientists are monitoring

species group of plants or animals that look and act the same way

stocked supplied

temperate not too hot or too cold

threatened group whose numbers are decreasing, bringing the group close to endangerment

thrive do very well

urban relating to the city

wetland very wet, low-lying area

More Books to Read

Barenblat, Rachel and Joan Craven. *Michigan the Wolverine State.* Cleveland: World Almanac Education, 2002.

Heinrichs, Anne. *Michigan.* Minneapolis: Compass Point Books, 2003.

Hintz, Martin and R. Conrad Stein. *Michigan.* Danbury, Conn.: Children's Press, 1998.

Johnson, Elizabeth M. *Michigan.* Danbury, Conn.: Children's Press, 2002.

Knox. Barbara. *Michigan.* Minnetonka, Minn.: Bridgestone Books, 2003.

Index

About the Author

Award-winning photographer and journalist Marcia Schonberg is the author of travel guides, nonfiction children's books, and the Heinemann Library Ohio State Studies books. She has contributed to *Michigan Living* and writes regularly for daily newspapers and regional and national magazines. A mother of three, Marcia resides in the Midwest with her husband Bill and golden retriever, Cassie.